I Have Seen It for Myself

An Eyewitness to the Power of God

Dr. Victor Morrell

ISBN 978-1-63630-347-5 (Paperback)
ISBN 978-1-63630-348-2 (Hardcover)
ISBN 978-1-63630-349-9 (Digital)

Covenant Books, Inc.
11661 Hwy 707
Murrells Inlet, SC 29576
www.covenantbooks.com

Dedication

This book is dedicated to the members and friends of Trinity Independent Baptist Church of Clinton, Maryland, whose love, diligence, determination, and devotion for the Lord has made this writing possible. You have been my source of joy and praise to God. Your steadfast and can-do spirit, along with your unceasing prayers and petitions before God has helped me more than you will ever know. Thank you for your many years of sacrifice, especially during those times of crisis. May the Lord bless and keep you because of your love for His servant.

And to my wife, Carol, who loves the Lord and has been a faithful helpmeet in all my endeavors and the very image of the woman of Proverbs 31: "For her price is far above rubies."

CONTENTS

Open thou mine eyes, that I may behold wondrous things out of Thy law.

AUTHOR'S NOTE

The ability to see is by far one of the greatest gifts given to man by God. To be able to perceive one's own self and his surroundings, not to mention the beauty of God's creation, is remarkable in and of itself.

It is with sight that we can navigate life's journey, making our way from one destination to another. We also use sight to assist us in our comprehension and understanding of matters and to help us in making decisions regarding all aspects of life.

While it is important to have physical sight, I believe it is just as important to have spiritual perception as well. To be able to not only behold the majestic beauty of God's handiwork, but to perceive the presence and workings of God in our lives and everyday issues.

All too often we live not knowing how and when God is working. This is not to say that we do not believe God is working, but we cannot place our finger on the time that He did work. It is with this thought that I want to write to you and to let you know of a particular time when I can give witness to the working of God in my life and that of others around me.

It was during this time and situation that the Lord began to open the eyes of many to His power and presence with His people. And to show that He is a very present help to all those that call upon Him, no matter what the situation.

It is my desire that the Lord will use this material to impact your personal life in a special way so that you and those around you might be drawn closer to Him and that you might give testimony in saying, "I Have Seen It for Myself."

INTRODUCTION

We are called and have been admonished by the scripture to walk by faith and not by sight (2 Cor. 5:7). The Christian life is a walk of faith, believing and trusting God, no matter what comes our way. But there are times when a visual perception of a matter helps to validate and strengthens one's faith in Christ.

It is one thing to have been told or to have read of a matter and yet another to have experienced it yourself. The Bible is replete with demonstrations of God's power and working in the lives of many so that they might have a clearer perception of His person. While these stories are numerous, the story of Elisha and his servant is one that comes to mind in 2 Kings 6. There the story is told of Elisha being surrounded by the Syrian army and with nowhere to go. Fearing the worst, the young man cries out in distress and wonders what they are going to do with this great horde of soldiers and chariots around them.

However, there was a calmness about Elisha. He knew that there was nothing to worry about because his eyes were open to the presence and power of God in his life. Because the young man was unable to see what Elisha saw, Elisha prayed that his eyes would be open so that he too would see God for himself.

> "And Elisha prayed, and said, Lord, I pray thee, open his eyes, that he may see. And the Lord opened the eyes of the young man; and he saw." (2 King 6:17)

What a remarkable change must have come over this young man. To see the presence and power of God for himself, I believe, enabled him to move beyond his present circumstances of panic and anxiety into a place of trusting and resting in his God. Why? Because he had his eyes open and has seen God for himself.

Another story deals with two men as they walked to Emmaus in Luke 24. The Bible tells that as these men walked to Emmaus, the Lord drew near and went with them. However, they were unable to recognize the risen Savior because "their eyes were holden that they should not know him" (v. 16).

These men had believed that Jesus would be the One to set Israel free from her captors and restore the kingdom in some mea-sure. They had been told by the women of seeing angels who testified that Christ was risen from the grave and was alive. However, because they were slow to believe, the Lord sought to expound to them from the scriptures all things concerning himself. As they heard his teachings, they desired that he would tarry with them because the day was far spent. However, the Bible says, "And it came to pass, as he sat at meat with them, he took bread and blessed it, and brake, and gave to them. And their eyes were opened, and they knew him" (vv. 30–31).

What a remarkable turnaround for these men. Though they had eyes to see the Lord physically but were blind to Him spiritually. It was not until their eyes were opened that they could truly comprehend the person and presence of the Lord and be an eyewitness to His resurrection. Hence, they had to see it for themselves.

Faith is the basis upon which everything is founded in the Christian faith. We are saved by it, admonished to walk by it, and told to live in a way that we have hope through it. And while faith is the basis of all that we stand on, there are times when the Lord has to open our eyes to see Him and what He is doing more clearly in order to increase our awareness of His presence.

While many of us have never experienced anything with the Lord on this level, it does not mean that God has not worked in our lives in a real way to make Himself known unto us. Our problem, like both the young man of Elisha's day and the two travelers on the Emmaus Road is that we are hard pressed to identify the moment God works in our lives. Often, it is after we have been through a situation that we notice only God could have engineered the circumstances for my deliverance and no other.

It will be our approach in this writing to testify that we have seen the hand of God working in a real and personal way in my life and the lives of those around me. In other words, there are others who are eyewitnesses to this fact and, if asked, could say, "I Have Seen It for Myself."

CHAPTER ONE

The Principles of Faith
(How We Ought to Walk)

I have found it is extremely easy to speak, hear, and read about faith, but it is a different thing to have it. How great is our faith when all is going our way, but what happens to it when the storm clouds grow darker and the fear of what might happen comes? Job said,

> "For the thing which I greatly feared is come upon me, and that which I was afraid of is come unto me" (Job 3:25).

It is quite easy to have faith when you are on the mountain top and all our cares seemed to be addressed. We seem to be counted among the faithful when our cupboards are full, our children are in safety, our careers are on the upward bound, and all of life's issues are a thing of the past. But I must remind you that the testing of faith is not when you are on the mountain top, but when you are in the valley. As matter of fact, for every mountain top experience, be prepared for a valley ambush. It is at this point that so many are given a reality check about their faith and whether it measures up or not.

The writer of Proverbs wrote: "If thou faint in the day of adversity, thy strength is small" (Prov. 24:10). The prophet Jeremiah writes,

> "If thou hast run with the footmen, and they
> have wearied thee, then how canst thou contend
> with horses? And if in the land of peace, wherein
> thou trustedst, they wearied thee, then how wilt
> thou do in the swelling of Jordan" (Jer. 12:5).

It is during the peaceful times that we forget to prepare our faith for the testing. It is when we believe all is clear that the trial and the challenges come. Even when we know to have faith, it is then that we have selective amnesia and forget that we are to have it.

It is in the time of the unexpected and the unknown, along with uncertainties, that challenges our faith the most. Even when we are supposed to be walking in it, we often find ourselves filled with doubts, reservations, and questions about God and His ability to help us in time of our needs. Life is never easy nor is it always fair. We find ourselves on top of the world one day, and the next, it seems, the world is on top of us.

Great Faith Must Have Great Trials

—*C. Spurgeon*

This is the testing of faith that I now speak of. One that challenges the very core of our being and the very fabric of our profession. It is here when the winds of life begin to blow contrary to our desires, we will either proclaim, like Job, "Though he slay me, yet will I trust in him" (Job 13:15). Or we will be like the apostles and ask, "Master, carest thou not that we perish?" (Mk. 4:38).

It is in these turbulent times of life that we find out what we are all about. Trials are indifferent to our status, position, or our prestige among men. They are an equal opportunity destroyer and will use any means necessary to expose us. Hence, they have a way of cutting through the false bravados and the eloquent but empty words and bring us to the forefront of our innermost person and to acquaint us to the (real) proverbial man in the mirror.

The apostles were to be season men of faith and character. Men who have seen the Lord work in a miraculous way. Did they not witness how the blind receive their sight? And were they not there when on countless occasions the lame was made to walk again? And were they not the distributors of the few loaves of bread and fish, that when He had blessed it, fed above five thousand? And did they not witness the power of the Lord when the widow's son, Jairus's daughter, and even Lazarus, their friend, was raised from the dead? No amount of storm should have shaken their faith, they should have never panicked in such a manner, but they did. And because they failed to walk by sight and not by faith, even though they were eyewitnesses to some of the greatest miracles by our Lord, he asked, "Why are ye so fearful? How is it that ye have no faith?" (Mk. 4:40).

> **"Sometimes, You Just Have To Bow Your Head, Say A Prayer AND Weather The Storm"**
>
> —*Author Unknown*

The matter of faith is at the center of all that we are and will be. It will determine our destiny and the road that we take. Our success and failures will depend upon it as it seeks to either guide us through our dilemmas or bring us to sure destruction because of the lack thereof.

It is because of the problem that we are going to face, that our faith will either stand or fall in midst of our troubles. We will either be drawn to God in a more powerful way to see Him more clearly or we will allow our situation to overcome us in the end whereby we are unable to see His power at work in our lives. It is not enough to say we have faith, there comes a time when our faith must carry us and not we carry it. For the storm does not always seek to destroy us, but on the contrary, it seeks to reveal and give evidence of the faith that we possess already. We are to have faith, but we must admit that there are times when our faith does not measure up when it should. The storm is coming and the question before us is "How strong is my faith?" I know that I am to have faith and to walk in it and what the

Lord expects of me, but I must cry out like the father of the demon possessed son cried,

> "And straightway the father of the child
> cried out, and said with tears, Lord, I believe;
> help thou mine unbelief" (Mk. 9:24).

CHAPTER TWO

The Problem Develops

1.   Gathering Clouds

In life there will be moments of sunshine, where everything is in harmony
and all is at rest. There are times when
the refreshing rains will come to water
and to grow you in pressing forward
in your faith and trust with the Lord.
And there are times when we see
the darkening skies and the thicken-
ing clouds which signals a storm is
coming.

Unlike Job, whose life was turned upside down in just a day, the
gathering clouds of my life would take on the ominous signs of darkening clouds over the course of months in the form of financial (real
estate) matters. Like a hurricane, which begins as a tropical depression (winds under 39 mph), my storm would develop slowly but
assuredly over time into a full-blown hurricane (winds over 74 mph)
that will seek to undermine my life and the lives of many around me.

The clouds began gathering about eighteen months ago when
there was a slowdown in the economy and our mortgage was being
transferred to a third-party vendor, who would require additional

adjustments in our payment to maintain our loan. This new salvo would be the first in the gathering storm that would change our days from one of gladness to a conscious uneasiness and anxiety regarding our future.

As time would have it, we would begin to see a change in the makeup of the clouds that constantly hovered over us; they became more darker and more threatening as the months passed. As a matter of fact, the storm had gotten to such intensity that it was in our best interest to obtain legal counsel to deal with the matter, hoping that we could prevent any further escalation of the situation—to which it did not. We sought every means to bring the ship to shore, but all our efforts were futile at best. All our resources were useless in the face of this juggernaut of a storm. Have you ever been in a situation where your efforts came up short?

It reminds me of a similar situation experienced by a widow in 2 Kings 4. There we read, "Now there cried a certain woman of the wives of the sons of the prophets unto Elisha, saying, Thy servant, my husband is dead; and thou knowest that thy servant did fear the Lord: and the creditor is come to take unto him my two sons to be bondmen" (2 Kings 4:1).

This poor widow had a financial storm that had gathered in her life. She had no means of repaying or meeting the family's obligation since her husband was now dead. This storm in her life had now intensified to the point the creditor was threatening to come and seize her sons to make them bondmen (slaves) until the debt was paid off. There was no mercy or compassion shown to this widow. No understanding of her situation, just a storm that has now developed and was beginning to pour down upon her. Have you ever been in this situation before? Have you ever had your back against the wall, and you could see no way out of your situation? And no matter how hard you cried, your cry seems to have fallen on deaf ears or on the hearts of the insensitive and uncaring.

I am reminded that the gathering clouds of life are never there to bring you comfort and joy, but turmoil, chaos, and confusion. They are not seeking your rest but just the opposite, your unrest and loss of peace. The clouds are gathering over your life, and it does not look like the clouds of a summer rain to nourish you and to grow you but are the signs of a storm that is coming to cause you harm and anxiety.

2.   Another Front Appears

There are times in our life when we are faced with one issue after another. It is one thing to contend with one matter until its conclusion and yet another to divide your focus and strength on simultaneous issues. When I look at the Bible, I find that Job was a man who had to deal with multiple fronts (trials) in his life.  One moment he hears about his herds being taken away and the next about all his children dying in a freak storm while they were in their eldest brother's house. What a day this must have been for Job. Before he could adjust himself to the sad news from one servant, up pops another with more disturbing and devastating news. That is life for you!

Just as the storm clouds of one issue had gathered over me, there would appear on the scene the presence of another cloud just as dark and ominous and even more demanding than the first. This cloud was not the results of financial inabilities or the pressures of others but would come from within and take the form of a reoccurring medical challenge called cancer.

It was during my usual doctor's visit that I was instructed to get my annual chest x-ray completed. Since my schedule was free for a few hours, I decided to walk downstairs and have the procedure completed. It was the next day when I received a call from my doctor asking me to come back in immediately to discuss a matter. Of course, I was curious to know what prompted this call for an immediate meeting and so I went to see him as directed.

It was once I arrived that he informed me that there was an unusual large mass in my chest near my lungs and other vital areas, and that I would need to get it checked out quickly to determine if it was cancerous. He immediately dispatched me to an oncologist hematologist, who when he examined me sent me to a thoracic surgeon that later determined the mass was possibly cancerous but could not be more definitive until surgery *(biopsy)* was performed.

From the time of the chest examination to the surgery was less than thirty days. I was placed under the knife (three small cuts on my side) while the surgeon went between my rib cage to extract the entire mass instead of a simple biopsy. After careful testing and examination, it was now definitive, the mass contains cancer cells, and based upon additional scans, the cancer had spread (metastasis disease) to my lymph node system. It was determined that I was in full-blown stage four cancer. To say that I was dumbfounded and bewildered would be the understatement of the year. Having gone through cancer before (some twelve years earlier), I was taken back and wondered what was coming next. As a matter of fact, I was told that usually at this stage, it was the normal procedure to just keep the patient comfortable and out of pain.

Because I was a previous cancer patient, the doctors ordered a series of tests and scans to be performed. However, the more tests they ran, the more the dark storm clouds seemed to be gathering over me. I was bounced from one exam to another, from one office to another. All parts of my body were subject to scans, even my bones and brain. And if that were not enough, and what made this whole episode astonishing, was the inability of the initial testing site to diagnose the type of cancer that I had developed. With this lingering issue, any treatment recommendation or suggestions had to be placed on hold until a more precise diagnosis could be determine.

Like Job, before I can grasp and get my hands around one matter, up comes another of a different kind but with the same aim: to test my faith for what sort it is. It would have been great to concentrate my faith on one issue at a time, I suppose that is not asking too much, is it? But sadly, I am reminded that life does not always play fair nor does it give us what we desire. Job had to fight with multiple issues in his life at the same time, shall we expect anything different? Are we to be counted special and not face the prospect of overwhelming odds and trials in our life? I think not. The storm clouds are gathering over you, but this time from a different area of life—are you ready? Can your faith handle more than one challenge?

3. Gaining Strength

It is one thing to have a storm upon you and another to have that storm grow in intensity and severity. One can only imagine how Job must have felt when his day would not get any better but grow worse. The storm clouds that came at first are now thick and seeking to level Job to the ground. Before a storm can be called a hurricane, it must move from a tropical  depression to a tropical storm first. It must have a certain level of increased and sustained winds to be classified as such.

Life storms when they are upon us simultaneously have the tendency to grow in strength and pressure. They seek to pull you from one side to another until you have exhausted your resources and strength. They reinforce themselves by feeding off one another until you are left wondering what to do and where to go. In 1 Samuel 13, the story is told of King Saul and Israel and their reaction to their battle with the Philistine army.

> "And the Philistines gathered themselves together to fight with Israel, thirty thousand chariots, and six thousand horsemen, and people as the sand which is on the seashore in multitude...When the men of Israel saw that they were in a strait, (for the people were distressed) then the people did hide themselves in caves, and

in thickets, and in rocks, and in high places and
in pits...and all the people followed him trembling" (1 Sam. 13:5–7).

Israel's problem did not go away nor did it succumb to a one-
time defeat brought by Jonathan but regathered and strengthened
itself to Israel's surprise. Life's problems do not go away simply
because you have a momentary victory but seem to be more intensified in bringing about our distress and destruction.

I was now battling two major issues in my life at one time and
it appears that they are in no way calming down but for all practical
purposes are getting stronger day by day. They are making unreason-
able demands—the one for my finances and the other my life—and,
no matter what I do, I am unable to satisfy either. The pressure is
growing. What am I to do with such a convergence of storms in my
life? How do I satisfy the ravenous appetite of the creditor who seeks
to take all that I and others have worked so hard to build? What am
I to say to the doctor who tells me at this stage, there is nothing for
us to do but keep you comfortable, because often at this stage, a life
is required? How can I get from up under the daily darkness that the
storms bring into my life and the lives of those around me? Houston,
we have a problem, and it looks like before it will get better, it will
most certainly get worse. The storms have strengthened in your life
and the question is what will you do? How will you deal with the
problems all around you? Will you hide in a cave? Will you be dis-
tressed and depressed because you can see no way out? Or will you be
afraid and trembling at the enormity of the situation? What?

No matter how bad and numerous our problems might be,
we must be determined to move forward. We cannot allow our problems to corral us into believing there is no solution to our situation.
Someone said that worrying is like a rocking chair, it will give you
something to do, but it will get you nowhere. While I recognized the
storms are gathering strength, I have a choice to make: stand or fall. I
cannot afford to sit on the sideline and allow the storms to cover me
with an attitude of doom and gloom. What will you decide?

Chapter Three

A Proposed Solution

I have a two-front problem in my life that is bearing down on me like a runaway semi-truck. The problem has touched the very thing I need the most and seeks to take more than I am willing to give. How do I eradicate myself of this menace to my household and to my life in general? Are there any solutions available that can rectify my anguish and relieve me of the daily pressures that have so easily overtaken others? Yes, I believe there are ways to handle problems when they arise in our life. However, the storms are not so easily persuaded to barter with me if it believes it has the upper hand.

In my case, I was desperately seeking a way to rectify both of my problems, even though they had their own level of difficulty and possible solution. On the one hand, it would take a simple restructuring of the books and the problem would be solved. A little creative financing here and

HOUSTON WE HAVE A SOLUTION

a little there and we would be in business. Hence, one problem was solved and put to bed. Or the property in question could be sold and the debt paid. All great solutions from my viewpoint. But the storm's aim is not to settle on my terms but its own. It has but one solution in mind: full absolution of the matter and nothing less and within a certain period. It was seeking to exact its pound of flesh at all cost. Have you ever had a viable solution to your problem nullified without due consideration and discussion? The writer of Proverbs reminds us of the character and temperament of the creditor when he wrote:

"The rich rule over the poor, and the bor-
rower is servant to the lender" (Prov. 22:7).

How can a solution be found if the lender loathes such arrogance over me and rejects even the simplest of solutions? Will not the storm break so that we might reason together to resolve this matter—the answer is an unequivocal *NO*. There will be no negotiations. The price has been set and nothing short of full payment now will satisfy. This is what sin demands of fallen man. It is all or nothing. There is no room for compromise; our best acts and suggestions will not do, it requires everything.

With the hope of my financial storm going unsatisfied and still looming over my head, I turned my attention to the other storm (medical) raging in my life. Here, it is not as simple to come up with a single fixed solution. Here, the gate to solutions is wide, and the way is broad and there are many elusive antidotes offered. There is no guarantee that the treatment selected will correct or solve the problem, it only gives you the illusion or veil disguise or promise of something better. It is this storm that we see a greater ravenous desires and aim: to separate me from that which is deemed a most precious gift, my life. It seeks to make my wife a widow and my children fatherless and me a past thought and memory.

Because of the seriousness of this disease, time was of the essence in selecting a treatment plan. My research on the matter yielded an infinite amount of treatment plans and solutions (immunotherapy, insulin therapy, proton beam therapy, chemotherapy) that could not be absorbed in a lifetime, and especially in the short time span that was given to me. It was overwhelming to say the least as I comb through one plan after another. To say that the pressure was great is an understatement. But here we are facing one of the most devastating illnesses that bring nothing but dread and fear at its very mention.

After all the research and discussions were completed, a course of action was decided and approved by the doctor and me. No one knows if this will work, seeing this is my second brush with cancer, but now it has metastasized and had free course within my body. The prognosis was not looking good at this point given the history of this type of cancer. But a decision has been made and we must continue to look forward despite the odds. I indicated to the doctor that no one would be dying today, especially not me due to this disease. I was believing that God would show himself mighty considering the evidence to the contrary.

The storm clouds have gathered, and the winds have strengthened themselves over the course of a short period of time I am now facing a two-front, full-blown hurricane in my life and every solution offered has either been rejected and/or reduced to a spin of the wheel. Nothing is certain at this point except the storm is raging and it is seeking its next victim.

Have you ever been in a position where nothing seems to work? And all your best laid plans are upended and are unable to stop the storm that blows in your life? What can we do when there are no solutions available, must we succumb to the overwhelming force of our trials? Is there no one to hear and help us as we are being engulfed by our trials and troubles?

I am reminded of a poem written by my wife that I believe helps during these difficult times and situations. It reads,

God Is Always There

When you think no one cares,
Just remember God is there.
When you are lonely and feeling blue
Just remember God will see you through.
When you can't reach the person you call,
Just remember God knows it all.

When you are sick and don't know what to do,
Turn it over to Jesus and he will work it out for
you.
When you can't find man to give you a helping
hand,
Pray to God because He understands.

—Carol Morrell

God
DOES NOT GIVE US WHAT
WE CAN HANDLE.

GOD
HELPS US HANDLE WHAT
WE ARE GIVEN.

—*Author Unknown*

CHAPTER FOUR

The Prayer of the Saints

What am I to do when my life is in an upheaval and trials seem to be my constant companion? How do I face the ever-present turmoil that seeks to destroy all that I and others have built, to see many years of hard work be threatened and on the verge of being taken away? What am I to do when life itself is in jeopardy and the thought of death permeates your mind daily? Where am I to turn when my best laid plans have been foiled, and instead being on top of the world, the world is constantly on top of me?

I am reminded in the Bible that the answer to man's problem is to be found in the person of Christ and soliciting His help by making our request known unto Him. We are to seek Him in every aspect of life and especially when the storms of life begin to rise and seek to consume or carry us away from Him.

> "For the **eyes** of the Lord are over the righteous, and His **ears** are open unto their prayers"
>
> *1 Peter 3:12*

I had two storms in my life raging simultaneously, and it looks like it was not getting any better but worse. I believe the best course of action at this point was to be engaged in earnest prayer and supplication before my God, the Lord Jesus Christ. While these storms may have been personal in nature, they also involved the lives of many others, whom if the storms were successful would be devastated. Because of this, I engaged God's people to join me in putting these matters before the Lord daily in their personal devotions and Bible reading. We are told in the Book of Acts that when Peter was kept in prison, "Prayer was made without ceasing of the church unto God for him" (Acts 12:5). It is through prayer that I begin to fight the storms in my life because when we pray God begins to work.

Though my storms were growing ever so threatening day by day, I went about selecting various passages of scripture that would help me to address the ills in my life and to keep me focused during these difficult times. I did not want to be engaged in prayer that was general in nature, but I wanted one that would be laser focused and direct given my unique situation. This is not to say there were no other items on my prayer list, but there were two problems that needed God's immediate attention.

One of the passages of scripture used in my prayers during this time is found in 2 Chronicles 20, verses 1–15. This passage of scripture helps me to understand what to do when one is facing overwhelming odds in their life. Here the armies of the Ammonites, the Moabites, and Edomites (Mt. Seir) were seeking to come against Jehoshaphat and the people of Judah to battle. The king, recognizing that this was an impossible situation, turned to seeking the Lord and proclaimed a fast throughout all Judah. The king understood that a storm was forming on his border and was poised to overcome him if nothing was done. But what could he do? He started his petition by asking God a series of questions that were rhetorical in nature but sought to validate what the king believed about God. Also, by his own admission he tells God, "O our God, wilt thou not judge them? for we have no might against this great company that cometh against us, neither know we what to do: but our eyes are upon thee" (v. 12).

Herein is a prayer I placed before God each day. I wanted God to know how much I believed in Him. I wanted Him to understand that I believe there was nothing on earth so great that He could not handle, because just like Jehoshaphat, I believe, "In thine hand is

28

there not power and might, so that none is able to withstand thee" (v. 6). It was in this prayer that I wanted God to know that I acknowledged my inabilities and insufficiencies to handle my storm. That I had no resources to rectify this situation and that all must come from Him. I wanted Him to know that my eyes were steadfast on Him and him alone in this crisis.

Another passage used during this time is found in 1 Kings 17:8–16 regarding Elijah and the widow woman. Here in this text I see the matter of trusting God when all seems impossible.

At this point in Israel's history, God had withheld the rain from the nation. You can only imagine what happens to an agrarian society when there is an absence of rain: no crops, no food, and the beginning of widespread starvation. And so, we find this woman gathering sticks one last time so that she might go home and prepare one last meal for her and her son. But now she meets Elijah and is challenged in her faith toward God when he said,

> "Go and do as thou hast said: but make me thereof a little cake first, and bring it unto me, and after make for thee and for thy son. For thus saith the Lord God of Israel, the barrel of meal shall not waste, neither shall the cruse of oil fail, until the day the Lord sendeth rain upon the Earth" (1 Kings 17:13–14).

One thing the storms of life are good at is keeping us from trusting God when all seems impossible. The setting of this story could have been more real to this woman because it touched the very thing she and her household needed the most: food. And now she is being asked to trust God even though there was no means of replenishing her cupboards or looking beyond the little meal and oil she had left. Wow. What was she going to do? What would you do when you are down to your last and there is no way to get more? Will you trust God at that moment or settle for the inevitable?

It was in this passage that I was reminded that God can take the little and do great things with it. He can take the impossible and make it possible, if only we trust Him. I wanted to let God know that while my life was filled with one setback after another and the way was not clear as to my outcome, I would trust Him, believing He could overcome the impossible. As a matter of fact, the Bible says, "For with God nothing shall be impossible" (Luke 1:27). To escape my storms, I needed to have a faith that believed, even during impossible times, that my situation can be overcome, that I could gain the victory. I was not going to allow my storms to rob me of what my God could do. I did not care if the clouds were growing more threatening as the days passed, I was going to believe, "The effectual fervent prayer of a righteous man (along with engaging God's people) availeth much" (James 5:16).

While the storms of life were raging and coming against me, the saints of God were praying for me. We had set our hearts to seeking the Lord in these matters and nothing was going to persuade us otherwise that God could not move on our behalf. It was our privilege and our duty to bombard the throne of God with our prayers and supplications. We are told to come and come we did (see Hebrews 4:16). For we were convinced that "the eyes of the Lord are over the righteous, and his ears are open unto their prayers" (1 Peter 3:12). I believe the best way to fight a two-front storm is by  using a simple but single approach, prayer. Someone said that, "When we work, we work. But, when we pray, God works" (unknown).

The storm is raging all around me, but I will continue to call on the name of the Lord because He has promised to hear and answer me in times of my need. Jeremiah writes,

> "Call unto me, and I will answer thee, and
> show thee great and mighty things, which thou
> knowest not" (Jer. 33:3).

I am also reminded of a poem entitled, "Going to God in Prayer" that tells the believer simply,

> Going to God in prayer because I know that He will always be there. When you pray look above because God wants to show you his special love. Don't give up, He is there. He will take you in his care. In His will, He will see you through, because He knows all about you. Just keep the faith and trust God because He wants to intervene for us. (Carol Morrell)

What a privilege it is to be able to carry our desires and burdens to the Lord. He wants to hear from us, if only we would seek Him when the storm clouds begin to arise in our life. We are told to cast our cares upon Him because He cares about us (see 1 Peter 5:7). Yes, we have problems in life, but praise be to God that we have a High Priest and Advocate who loves to hear from His people and intervene for them. My friend, whatever you are wrestling with today, take it to God in prayer. Stay at His feet with your cries night and day until he answers. Let Him know that you will not faint, even when the winds blow much harder and your days become darker. The psalmist wrote, "What time I am afraid, I will trust in thee" (Ps. 56:3). Also, the prophet Isaiah writes, "Thou wilt keep him in perfect peace, whose mind is stayed on thee: because he trusted in thee" (Isa. 26:3).

We cannot win these battles on our own, we need the power of God to be involved. Only He can turn our situation around and bring us through the storms of life. He is waiting for you and me to come to Him. Do not spend another moment battling your issues or seeking how to get out of your storm. Why not resolve today that you will give it all to Him through prayer. He is waiting. Will you come?

"Come unto me, all ye that labour and are heavy laden, and I will give you rest. Take my yoke upon you, and learn of me; for I am meek and lowly in heart: And ye shall find rest unto your souls. For my yoke is easy, and my burden is light" (Matt. 11:28–30).

CHAPTER FIVE

The Power of God Visualized

All too often we become so fixated on the storm that we forget to see the workings of God in our lives. It is easy to lose focus when the dark clouds of trouble arise, especially on many fronts. I am reminded of Israel and their journey out of Egypt to the Red Sea. The scripture is clear that as they left Egypt, God set before them a pillar of cloud by day and a pillar of fire by night. He wanted to give them a visual picture of his presence with them as they journeyed.

> "And the Lord went before them by day in a pillar of a cloud, To lead them the way; and by night in a pillar of fire, to give them light; to go by day and night. He took not away the pillar of cloud by day, nor the pillar of fire by night, from before the people" (Ex. 13:21–22).

Even when the threat of Pharaoh's chariots was coming upon them (see Exodus 14:5–10), the pillar of cloud and the pillar of fire remained with them so that they would have a visual symbol of God to anchor them against the pending storm. There was no need for them to be fearful and afraid because God had placed a visual representation of His power and presence with them.

The Bible is replete with visual demonstrations of God's presence and power to His people, especially when they faced challenging and demanding times in their lives. When I read about Gideon, I read about someone who wanted to confirm God's calling and presence in his life. And, because he wanted to make sure, the Lord allowed a visual demonstration of power before Gideon through two distinct tests (see Judges 6:36–40).

I can also tell you of Elijah on Mount Carmel and the great challenge he wroth before the people. The nation of Israel had become a people straddling the fence in their worship and indifferent to the God of their fathers. Elijah wanted to show them who the One true God was and would need a visual demonstration of God's power to convince the people of such. It was when the fire of God came down and consumed the sacrifice and the altar that we read,

> "And when all the people saw it, they fell
> on their faces: and they said. The Lord, he is the
> God; the Lord, he is the God" (1 Kings 18:39).

A final story that comes to mind is the resurrection of Lazarus from the dead. This story is remarkable and unlike others that were raised by our Lord because he had been buried for four days. Here again, we see the need to have a clear demonstration of God's presence and power to be seen by those that stood by. John writes as the Lord prayed saying,

> "Father, I thank thee that thou hast heard
> me. And I knew that thou hearest me always: But
> because of the people which stand by I said it,

That they may believe that thou hast sent me"
(John 11:41–42).

There are times when God will give us a visual demonstration of His presence and power. He knows there are moments, especially when trials come, that we may need to see Him working in a real way. Again, this is not to say that we do not believe He is working, but there are times we need to pinpoint when He is working on our behalf.

As my storms grew in intensity and the pressures mounted, consuming both my time and energy, I and many others pressed ourselves forward in prayers and petitions to God. Believing that God would do something to alleviate the situations that had befallen me once and for all.

As the days passed, the storms began to converge on me and were coming to a head—on the one hand all financial transactions were to be completed in less than a week and a half. There were to be no further discussions or forbearance of the matter. No ifs, ands, or buts. The legal teams of all parties were positioning themselves for a knock down drag out fight, which at this moment was not going in our favor. We had promises made by others, but they failed through for one reason or another. And what we had on the table was falling short of the mark. We needed a miracle; we needed God to show himself mighty on our behalf; anything short of a visual representation of His presence and power would be useless and futile at best.

On the other hand, the other storm was beginning to flex its muscles. I had undergone several months of chemotherapy treatment, and now the time had come to test those treatments. The doctor ordered scans and tests of every kind to determine if progress has been made in eradicating my body of the enemy within. We needed to know if there was any relief seen in my lymph node system or if the cancer has increased. The test will reveal to us something, but no one knows until after the tests are completed. Either way, the inevitable awaits me.

A loss in any one of these storms would prove devastating to all concerned and especially to me. As I await the conclusion of the matters before me, I was reminded that as a child of God things would not be easy. That the road before me is paved with one struggle after another. That nothing good will come without a cost.

As a matter of fact, the Bible tells me,

> "Many are the afflictions of the righteous: But
> the Lord delivereth him out of them all" (Ps. 34:19).

and

> "Yea, and all that will live godly in Christ
> Jesus shall suffer persecution" (2 Tim. 3:12).

Like Gideon and Elijah, a visual demonstration of God's presence and power would be welcomed at this stage of my life. To have the Lord of glory step in and show Himself mighty would be all right with me. But I asked myself this, "Has God given me any signs to show me He is working?" Has He been behind the scenes working as the writer of Romans indicated when he wrote,

> "And we know that all things work together
> for good to them that love God, to them who are
> the called according to his purpose" (Rom. 8:28).

Could He be working out my storms just as he worked out the storms in the life of Joseph? Could He be preparing me for something greater, but the storms are needed to get me ready for the next step? I remind you that Joseph went through a series of trials before he could be second in command over all Egypt. He was sold into slavery by his brothers, falsely accused by Potiphar's wife, and overlooked by Pharaoh's servant while in prison before he stood before Pharaoh's throne. What hardships he endured. But remembered what he said to his brethren at the end,

"But as for you, ye thought evil against me;
but God meant it unto good" (Gen. 50:20).

Joseph recognized that God was working behind the scenes on his behalf. As each chapter of his life opened, God was there to make sure that Joseph found grace in the sight of those around him. He did not understand every aspect of what God was doing, but somewhere along the line, Joseph knew that God was working and giving him a visual demonstration of His presence and power in his life.

I wonder how many of us see God working in our storms. Do we see His mighty hand engineering our circumstances so that the storm, no matter how dark and threatening, will not overcome us? Do we see Him working in your life in a manner whereby you also might say, "I have seen it for myself"?

Life is filled with many chapters. There are times when our lives are engulfed in suspense and intrigue, and, there are times when we cannot understand the reason behind some circumstances; we call that mystery. But it is another chapter that seems to fill our lives the most, and we called that chapter drama. It can appear at any time, any place, and involve many things, but it always touches that which we hold near and dear or need the most.

I am persuaded that though life contains many chapters, the last chapter has not been written yet. No one could have imagined Joseph's life ending the way it did, especially his brothers, Potiphar, or the king's butler. No one doubt Joseph's life was filled with mystery, intrigue, suspense, and drama, but because God was in the picture, we see a final chapter called happily ever after or victory.

This is the chapter I believe God would get me to in dealing with the storms of my life. For now, the drama and intrigue are rising, but so too is the presence and power of my God. The storm clouds are darkening all around me attempting to block any light of hope and deliverance, but it is in the darkest hour and the most tempestuous storms that my God shines the brightest.

Like Joseph and many others, the last chapter of our lives have not been written. And like Joseph, I too will testify in the end that what the storms meant for evil, my God will bring about for my good and declare, I have seen it for myself.

CHAPTER SIX

Prepared Outcome

As Israel entered the wilderness questions arose as to whether God could provide for them in such a barren place. As a matter of fact, they said, "Can God furnish a table in the wilderness" (Ps. 78:19)? They had seen and did testify that God did work in a miraculous way and brought water out of the rock, but now the circumstances have changed—can He work again (see Ps. 78:20)? Herein is where we are called upon and must walk by faith and not by sight. To believe that even when my circumstances change and the storm winds are at full strength, that God can stretch forth His hand and provide for us. In his writing to the church at Ephesus, the apostle Paul writes,

> "Now unto him that is able to do exceeding
> abundantly above all that we ask or think, accord-
> ing to the power that worketh in us" (Eph. 3:20).

Their outcome did not depend on God's abilities, but on them believing that God could provide for them, even in the harshest of conditions and circumstances. I wonder how many of us really believe God can bring us through our dilemma. Do we believe He can provide, even when there appears to be no way out or solution given?

It was on a Thursday morning that I will never forget. I was out mowing the lawn and decided to check my phone for calls and texts. To my surprise, my agent, who was now in another country, tried reaching out to me, but because of the mower, I was unable to hear the phone ring. By the grace of God, he had the ability to receive calls while out of the country, and so I was able to get the latest update.

It was then that I learned that a possible solution was reached by all the parties involved (legal teams across the country), but several documents needed to be signed immediately in order for the process to proceed and to meet the creditors demands and deadline. But upon checking, I informed the agent that no documents had been forwarded to me. A quick call to the broker indicated that he had not seen the files and 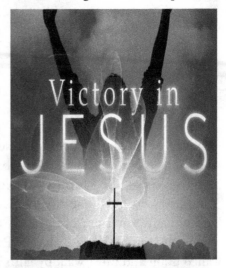 was unaware that they had been sent to him for his review and subsequent submission to me. As the storm clouds continued to gather their strength, now in the form of threats of court action, I was beginning to see the hand of God working through my situation. It was less than twenty-four hours earlier that all was in chaos and confusion. Crashing and burning were the only option before me, except the hand of the Lord guide the process. And to my delight, He did.

By Thursday evening, a remarkable thing had happened, the matter had reached a satisfactory closure for all involved. The warring parties that were adamant in their position and what they wanted were now put to bed and singing from the same sheet of music. And what a great melody it was to my ears. The call I received that evening told me that a date has been established to close the deal and that they wanted to know what time I would be available to come in.

Could there be any sweeter words to hear to the weary soul who has been under the storm clouds for so long?

I am a witness to the hand of God working and answering the prayers of His people. To know that only God could have orchestrated a one hundred eighty-degree turnaround between all the parties involved, especially in the proverbial ninth hour. To bring together individuals and organizations from across the country, with different time zones and objectives (California, Chicago, Virginia, and Maryland) was nothing short of a miracle. Instead of losing it all, I and many others stood to gain that which many presumed would be taken away. What a day to see God work in such a manner that all who stood by recognize that it was Him and no one else. It was He that turned the hearts of the creditor and also brought in a cash buyer who wanted to move with lightning speed to possess the property and to have a people who stood unwavering and steadfast believing and trusting that the Lord did not bring them this far to fall nor to lose it all. The psalmist wrote,

> "I waited patiently for the Lord; and he
> inclined unto me, and heard my cry. He brought
> me up also out an horrible pit, out of the miry
> clay, And set my feet upon a rock" (Ps. 40: 1).

It is He that deserves the honor and the glory for the great thing he has done unto me (and for us). For He heard our prayers and saw the tenderness of our hearts and steadfast spirit in this matter and decided by His own free will to intervene on our behalf. I have seen God work before, but because of the nature and the longevity of this problem, it was amazing to be an eyewitness to the presence and power of God in bringing this matter to a close in our favor. What a wonderful God He is and that we serve.

To allow such lowly creatures to approach His throne and to ask of Him the desires of their heart. For I can truly testify that I have seen God work for myself. How about you, my friend, have you ever seen God work in your life? Have you seen a demonstration of His awesome power at work turning your dark clouds into bright sunshine? Then, if you have the courage He is still working. He is still bringing his people through. And rest assured, He will see you through until the end that you might say like Israel,

> "When the Lord turned again the captivity of Zion, we were like them that dream. Then was our mouth filled with laughter, and our tongue with singing: Then said they among the heathen, the Lord hath done great things for them. The Lord hath done great things for us; whereof we are glad" (Ps. 126:1–3)

And glad we were that day. To leave the attorney's office with a new song of rejoicing in our heart and a new step in our walk. To see how God worked through our storms was a marvelous sight to behold and that we praised Him for the goodness and mercy that He had shown toward us.

I have been a witness to the hand of the Lord putting to rest one of the great storms in my life. And it's my belief that He would continue to work until all my storms are at an end. I

While you are praying, God is Working.

have made it through the first of my storms, allow me a moment to tell you what God did in the second.

While my first storm dealt with the matter of finances, it is the second storm that hit home with greater fierceness and possibility of doing the most harm because it dealt with life itself. But God, the keeper of all that is good and righteous, was still working behind the scenes all things for my good and for His glory.

After several months of chemotherapy treatment (six treatments), it was decided that a CT scan should be taken to ascertain information regarding the effectiveness of the treatment itself. To the doctor's amazement, the latest scan showed a significant reduction of the cancer in my lymph node system and elsewhere in my body. Based upon these findings, the doctor ordered the four remaining treatments (ten in total) to be given. What a great joy it was to hear those words. And how it was a far cry from the initial diagnosis received: to keep me comfortable. God was working.

After the remaining treatments (several more months have now passed) were administered, the doctor ordered the appropriate scans of the initial areas where the cancer was first detected. Several weeks passed before an appointment was set and to discuss the results. As I approached that day, many things went through my mind, but I must say none were of failure or dread. As a matter of fact, when my wife and I met with the doctor, before he could get in the door good, I told him the only thing I wanted to hear was praise the Lord for what great thing He has done. It was at that time the doctor said, "Well, I guess you better praise Him because there was no cancer detected." Praise the Lord for His kindness and endless mercies and for hearing the prayers of his people. What a mighty God we serve!

This makes the second time I have heard those words, but this time, it was much sweeter because of the fact I was labeled a stage-four cancer patient. It was not expected of me to beat cancer this time, only to live out the remainder of my days in comfort. But when man gives a death notice, God can give life and give it more abundantly.

I am reminded of the story, in the Gospel of John, chapter 11, between the Lord and Martha, after the death of her brother Lazarus. Martha believed that if the Lord had been there, their brother would not have died. But the Lord told Martha that her brother would rise again. She had taken this to mean that he would get up on the last day and not right now. Herein, is where the Lord challenges her faith by letting her know He is the resurrection and do she believe that. Her response was, "Yea, Lord: I believe." Later that day at the grave of her brother, the Lord commanded that the stone be rolled away. But it was Martha who objected to this move, seeing that her brother had been dead for four days already. All she could see was the natural order for all men: death. She could not see that the Lord of glory had power over death and the grave and that He was ready to show himself mighty to all that were around. I am quite sure that there was no objection from Lazarus about the stone being removed. I bet he was one happy camper to know that someone decided to obey the Lord and push back the stone.

INSTEAD OF GOING UNDER, WE CAME OUT ON TOP

The storms that ravished my life and demanded so much of my attention have now been relegated to just a soft summer breeze. The once fierce storms that sought to test my faith, and the faith of others, were now behind us and a thing of our past. Just when it looked like nothing would work and all our efforts proved to be futile at best, God stepped in and brought about a different outcome. Instead of going under, we came out on top. Instead of failure, we experience success. Instead of doubt and reservations, we stood and trusted God to the end.

The apostle Paul wrote to the Corinthian church,

> "We are troubled on every side, yet not destressed; we are perplexed, but not in despair; persecuted, but not forsaken; cast down, but not destroyed" (2 Cor. 4:8–9).

In other words, we might go down, but we will not stay down. The child of God is not immune to the trials of life nor can he be perfected without those trials. Paul also wrote when dealing with storms in his own life these encouraging words,

> "Most gladly therefore will I rather glory in my infirmities, that the power of Christ may rest upon me. Therefore, I take pleasure in infirmities, in reproaches, in necessities, in persecutions, in distresses for Christ sake: for when I am weak, then I am strong" (2 Cor. 12:9–10).

44

There is a time when we must stop carrying our faith and allow our faith to carry us. It is one thing to believe when all is well and there are no obstacles and hindrances in your way. But what will you do when the storms begin to form over you? How will you react when your days start to become dark and threatening and there appear to be no possible solution to your problem? Do you turn and give up or stand no matter how much the wind blows?

Fighting above the clouds in order to pass over the storm.
After being tossed to and fro while in the foggy blue skies.
For there is a brighter side on the other side.
For there are no rain drops nor rushing winds that blow.
So, let the sunshine in,
For it will truly be a victorious win.
After passing over the storm, the Lord will bring you through.
—Passing Over the Storm by Carol Morrell

There are choices to make and decisions to stand on. Will I allow my storms to get the best of me, or will I take notice of the work that God wants to do, if only I believe and trust Him? It takes the eye of faith to walk with God even when you cannot see Him working. For it is faith that says, "Though I do not see God, I believe that he is working all things for my good. I will make it through this storm, no matter how long it takes or how hard it becomes. And like the prophets and apostles of old, I too will stand and say aloud and with all confidence, I know that God is working in my life to better me and not break me. For I have seen it for myself."

CHAPTER SEVEN

Devotional
Drawing Closer to God

The Recognition of Who God Is
(Isaiah 6:1)

I believe that for someone to develop a closer relationship with God, there must first be a true recognition of the person of God.

Our society today has relegated God to nothing more than a cosmic errand boy, whose main mission is to be subservient to and heed our every beckoning call. Others have concluded that He is nothing more than an all-encompassing and all-powerful force that must be reckoned with. Yet there are still others who fashion God after the wicked imaginations of their own hearts, like those individuals mention by Paul in his writings to the Romans when he wrote:

> "Because that, when they knew God, they glorified Him not as God...But became vain in their imaginations, and their foolish hearts was darkened" (Romans 1:21).

If God was seen in the same light of biblical teaching for who He is, then we would be eager to develop a deep reverence for Him as a person. This is incredibly important for those who have professed the Lord as their personal Savior. Surprisingly, a few Christians are very repose in their lifestyles and personal walk with God probably because of their devaluation of Him to just a little more than a personal experience.

The prophet Isaiah gives us a clear and concise perspective as to how we can develop a closer walk with the Lord. In chapter 6, Isaiah was privileged to a profound event that would forever alter his relationship with God. The Scripture says that,

> "In the year that king Uzziah died I saw also the Lord sitting upon a throne, high and lifted up, and his train filled the temple" (Isaiah 6:1).

For Isaiah to fully appreciate and better understand his relationship with God, the Lord allowed the prophet to see an unusual vision concerning His Deity. This is not saying that the prophet was absent of any recognition of God, but now his eyes were open to the true reality of God's position, power, providence, and person.

When we begin to see God in his rightful position as the One who is the True and Living God, then we would not be as hasty to subjugate Him to our level or treat Him like "one of the boys." If we are to draw closer to the Lord, we must see him as the only true deity and nothing less.

> *If God was seen in the same light of biblical teaching for who he is, then we would be eager to develop a deeper reverence for him as a person.*

In recognizing God's deity, I believe that Isaiah also acknowledged God's power and providence over all creation by noting that He is "high and lifted up" and that "the whole earth is full of His glory." The apostle Paul substantiated this claim by writing: "For by him were all things created...and by him all things consist" (Col. 1:16–17). Thus, it would seem appropriate that the angelic host surrounding the throne would pay obeisance to God in a substantial way.

To draw close to God, there must be a proper recognition of His person. The prophet Isaiah understood this vision in its totality and viewed it as a vital link in developing a closer relationship with God. I hope that we will never take for granted God's position and come to recognize that our spiritual development will never proceed beyond this foundational belief.

The question then becomes, "Do you fully understand who God is? How about His position, providence, and power?" Why not start today by recognizing God for who he is—apart from the blessing that he has bestowed upon you. Remember that the first step in drawing closer and developing a more personal relationship to God is a proper recognition and placement of God in our lives.

The Recognition of Self
(Am I That Bad Off?)
(Isaiah 6:5)

We have seen that the first step in drawing closer to God begins with a right recognition of who God is. The prophet Isaiah had a better understanding about the position, power, providence, and person of God after seeing such a historic vision when he wrote, "...I saw also the Lord sitting upon a throne, high and lifted up, and his train filled the temple" (Isaiah 6:1). This enlightening experience by Isaiah appears to be the backdrop to what, I believe, is the second step needed in drawing closer to God and can be found in verse 5 of chapter 6, "Then said I, Woe is me! For I am undone; because I am a man of unclean lips." I believe the second step needed in drawing closer to God is proper recognition of one's self.

Immediately upon the receipt of this vision, Isaiah recognized his own self-worth and concluded that his life amounted to nothing more than "filthy rags" in light of the perfect holiness of God. This self-affirmation could not be done or understood until he first recognized God. This point is clearly seen in his reiteration of the events of verse one with the saying in verse five, "For mine eyes have seen the King, the Lord of host."

It is not always easy for people to recognize their state or to understand just how bad off they are. Yet every person who confessed Christ as their Lord and Savior has had to acknowledge their state before God, which is one of total depravity, due to the sin of our father Adam. However, the difficulty comes not in our recognition of this single fact, but in our failure to understand that we are, by nature, sinful creatures who, without the power of God, would immediately and without the least hesitation return to our erring ways.

The development of a closer relationship with God begins with the proper understanding of who we are as an individual. We must come to realize that our actions and activities may not always align themselves with the Word of God, and our persistence justification of our actions only seek to prove that we are "undone." Moreover, our improper evaluation of ourselves, along with the inability to admit our wrongs, constrains and hinders many Christians from ever developing a personal and sustaining relationship with God. Hence, our continual acceptance of those things, which we know are contrary to the Word of God, can never bring a holy God and us together. We must always be mindful of Isaiah's position, after being exposed to the awesome spectacle of God's position, power, providence, and person that God cannot dwell or commune with those who are unholy or seek to remain in a sinful state.

> *Moreover, our improper evaluation of ourselves, along with the inability to admit our wrongs, constrains and hinders us from ever developing and sustaining a relationship with God.*

The bottom line to what we have said thus far lies in the fact that our closeness to God is determined by our perception of who He is and our proper position in light of this understanding. Better yet, ask yourself the following questions:

1. What is my perception of God?
2. Is your perception according to the Bible or based upon your own views?

3. Considering your understanding of God, do you afford Him the proper reverence or respect?
4. Do you believe God can be approached with sin?
5. How do you view yourself considering your understanding of God?
6. Do you base your perception of self upon a proper view of God?
7. Can you develop a closer and personal relationship with God in lieu of your recognition of God and self? Why or Why not?

To draw closer to God, you and I must understand the importance of proper self-evaluation. The Holy Spirit of God makes known the position, power, and providence of a holy and righteous God to all mankind. However, it is up to us to recognize them as such. In addition, He also makes known to us our state before God (one of sin) and the need to confess that every man is in a state of deprivation due to sin.

I hope that you come to recognize your state before God, i.e., one that is totally inadequate before a holy and righteous God and that our subsequent cry should be like that of the prophet, "Woe is me!" Our inability to draw close to God depends on how we as a people look at ourselves. Without a proper recognition of self, a person can never develop a close and personal relationship with God. I hope that you will come to understand this as you strive for a better relationship with Him. Remember, it should be our desire to want to behold the beauty and majesty of the Lord and to be able to say, "I have seen it for myself."

Surrender:
(A Necessary Step)
(Acts 9:1–6)

In our journey thus far, we have determined that one's perspective regarding a proper knowledge of God, i.e., His position, power, and providence is necessary for the development of any relationship with Him. We also found that unless we recognize our standing before God as one of total inadequacy, trying to develop a relationship with Him would only prove to be inappropriate and unbefitting to a holy and righteous God. In lieu of this awareness, I believe that the third step needed for us in drawing closer to God is determined by whether we have totally surrendered to Him.

Because God created man with a free will that allows him to make decisions for himself, it is necessary for each of us to subject that free will to the will of God. This is by no means an easy task, given our sin nature. We are always quick to assert our claim to independence without giving any honest regard to how our independence or free will might affect our relationship with God. Far too often, it is not hard to find Christians who give the appearance of being sold out for Christ, but they often reserve a portion of their lives to themselves. This way of thinking has alienated many from developing a right relationship with God and consequently goes against the very Word of God and what he wants for us.

The Bible is replete with individuals who fail to recognize the preeminence of God in their lives and the need for proper submission to His will. On the other hand, however, the Bible does supply enough examples of strong-willed individuals who recognized the person of the Lord and subjected themselves to His will in their daily lives. One such individual was Paul (formerly Saul of Tarsus).

Paul was an extraordinary individual who was very prominent in the Jewish religion. His loyalty to Judaism caused him to clash with everything disseminated by Christ and later preached by his disciples. It is clearly seen that Paul's intent was to crush this new religious phenomenon that was sweeping through Jerusalem and throughout Judaea, says Luke when he wrote: "And Saul, yet breathing out threatenings and slaughter against the disciples of the Lord, went unto the high priest" (Acts 9:1). You can only imagine the strong will and determination exhibited by Paul in carrying out his desires against God's people. Yet the Bible records some remarkable words concerning Paul and his encounter with the resurrected Christ in Acts 9:6: "And he trembling and astonished said, Lord, what wilt thou have me to do?"

Each born-again believer has had an encounter with the resurrected Christ. I am not saying that it is in the same manner experienced by Paul, but this experience should be to the point where it yields similar results. This once enviable man, who was strong in personal stance and belief, persecutor of Christ's church, has now surrendered his will to the very person he once denounced. The remarkable change experienced by Paul included no protracted transformation of time or years of theological training, but a heartfelt conviction that caused him to recognize himself and the need to submit (surrender) his total person to the will of God.

As a necessary step in drawing closer to God, you and I must come to understand that surrendering of our will is vitally important. Why not take a moment and observe what is happening here and see how the thought of surrendering is applicable to your personal life—the apostle Paul did.

Complete surrender to God, especially by God's own people, is one of the least things spoken of in the church and yet, it is the very thing that is needed the most. Any reservation that we tend to preclude to ourselves bars us from saying: "What wilt thou have me to do." For us to draw closer to God and become intimate with Him, we must become completely beholden to His will and not our own. God demands and expects complete and unconditional surrender from all those who desire to follow Him. There can never be two captains over our lives: God and self.

If you have not surrendered your life to the will of God, why don't you take a moment and ask God to help you in surrendering your life, will, children, spouse, decisions, talents, treasures, etc., to Him to be used as He sees fit in furthering His plan and program through you. Believe me, once total surrender has been declared, a closer and more personal relationship with the Lord can be developed and achieved. The apostle Paul, who was once driven by his own passions and desires to destroy the church, later wrote the following regarding surrendering to the Romans:

> "I beseech you therefore, brethren, by the mercies of God, that ye present your bodies a living sacrifice, holy, acceptable unto God, which is your reasonable service. And be not conformed to this world: but be ye transformed by the renewing of your mind, that ye may prove what is that good, and acceptable, and perfect will of God" (Romans 12:1–2).

Have you surrendered your will to the will of Almighty God? Have you given Him full control over your life and all that you have under your control? Remember, to draw closer to God and develop a personal relationship with him, you must surrender your will to Him as a necessary step in the process.

Obedience:
(A Prerequisite)
(1 Samuel 15:22–23)

As we have seen, the steps to drawing closer to God involves some intricate but necessary understandings that must be ascertained first before a real relationship can begin. Our understanding of His person will help us to understand His position, power, and sole providential authority over the world, which has subsequent bearing regarding our personal lives as well. Moreover, it is imperative that we come to see that our position before Him is one of depravity and sinfulness, and any attempt to build a relationship with Him, based upon our own righteousness, will certainly be encountered with a strong denunciation (judgment) and rebuke. In addition, it must be noted that without complete surrendering of one's own personal will to the headship and authority of Christ, one could never expect that a more meaningful and personal relationship will ever be properly engaged. Yet I believe that our next step in drawing closer to God lies with one's obedience to the total will of God.

It would seem somewhat ambiguous to write on obedience in lieu of our previous chapter on surrender. It is imperative for us to understand that the matters of total surrender in and of itself involve obedience. One could easily reach this stance, but for the most part, many Christians have never surrendered completely to God; therefore, obedience has been made to be nothing more than just a proverb that is spoken of in passing. One of the greatest hindrances in Christendom today is the philosophical belief that surrender and obedience should be treated as distinct but close cousins and not as Siamese twins.

As natural parents, we know the importance of obedience in the lives of our own children as they pertain to our own governing rules. How many parents would give anything to have a child that is totally obedient in carrying out their wishes and desires, as they are in the Lord? Doesn't obedience help to foster a deeper and a more personal relationship with the child who willingly obeys you as opposed to a child who is constantly bucking and kicking against your authority? Come now and let us be honest with ourselves for just a moment. Would not time be better spent developing a relationship with a child in obedience as opposed to a child knee deep in correction and punishment? I am not saying that a parent should spend more time with one child over the other, but how much more can be accomplished if obedience is already present in the child as opposed to a disobedient child who needs correction in order to obtain obedience?

Well, God, who is our heavenly Father, feels the same way. This does not mean that parents who have disobedient children should love them any less, but a more loving and personal relationship could never be nurtured in or around an atmosphere which contrasts the children desires against those of the parent.

> *God says that obedience is vitally important for the development of any personal relationship between Him and his children.*

God says that obedience is vitally important for the development of any personal relationship between Him and his children. This principle is clearly manifested in the first book of Samuel, chapter 15 between King Saul and Samuel the prophet. According to this passage, God commanded Saul to destroy the Amalekites in their entirety, including all livestock. Yet we find in this narrative that Saul was not totally obedient to the will of God and decided to make a few adjustments to God's order (1 Sam. 15:8–9). If that were not enough, when approached by the prophet Samuel in verses 13–14 about the noise that he had heard, Saul attempted to defend his action by reverting to his love for God and blaming others for his failures to carry out God's will. Yet the prophet Samuel posed one question (v.22) to the disobedient king that should underscore God's viewpoint regarding obedience and, consequently sealed Saul's fate and kingship, and should be an indispensable lesson unto us even today:

> "Hath the Lord as great delight in burnt offerings and sacrifices, as in obeying the voice of the Lord?"

You can just imagine the look on Saul's face when he contemplated what he had planned to do for God with the animals he had captured from the Amalekites. Saul soon discovered that all his good intentions are never a sufficient reason for disobeying God. And thus, he was rejected as the king of Israel.

How many of us today are hindering God from having a closer relationship with Him because of our disobedience to His Word. We may have all the right intentions, but if it is contrary to what God commands, then we are disobedient to Him, which subsequently hinders our relationship to Him.

As children of God, how can you expect to be closer to God when you go contrary to what He has commanded? It is not enough for us to be given the Word of God, like that of Saul, and yet not adhere to its every precept. Is our life like that of Saul? Are you living a disobedient life before God? Do you hear the Word of God, but because of your own personal pride and stubbornness, you refuse to obey? Maybe you are considering a decision or are already engaged in some activity that you know is wrong before God—the question is, do you care what God thinks?

No matter what the reason or excuse we conjure up in order to justify our actions, we must understand that the development of a closer relationship with God requires total obedience on our part. No

Christian can ever expect to become closer to a Holy and Righteous God and to draw close to Him when He looks upon our disobedience as sin (see 1 Samuel 15:23).

Take a moment and look at your life; is it a life of obedience or disobedience? If you find that it is the latter, why don't you fall to your knees and ask God's forgiveness about your rebellious attitude and/or actions and help you learn how to submit to His will in your life.

Drawing closer to God requires us to obey Him in all our being, anything less only seeks to draw us further away from His person. We must always remember that obedience is a prerequisite in drawing closer to God, and that God delights and will honor those who obey his commands, which are given to us through His written Word. (Read Exodus 5:1–2; Jeremiah 7:23–24).

The Word
(The Knowledge of God)
(Romans 10:17; 1 Peter 2:2)

Our road to drawing closer to God has had many integral parts, which allows for the facilitation of one desired purpose—a closer and more personal relationship with God. This is achieved first by recognizing the divine deity of God and, second, by acknowledging our frail and deprive state before Him. Moreover, it was also determined that God expects complete subservience to His headship (and will) by those who would draw closer to Him—total surrender and obedience. And to offer Him anything less would only seek to hinder us in developing our relationship with Him. In lieu of what has been discussed thus far, I believe that the next step needed in drawing closer to God is centered in our knowing Him personally through His Word.

Relationships between individuals are built upon the fundamental premise of knowing and understanding the likes and dislikes of the individual. Regardless of the type of relationship that one seeks to establish—business, sports, casual, or the life-long commitment of marriage—there must be interaction between the parties involved in order to allow for discovery of personal facts about one another. This does not mean that increased knowledge automatically leads to the establishment of a personal relationship but that the ability to decide whether to have one will be greatly enhanced due to the newly acquired information.

Of course, you and I can never treat God like one of the boys, but the principle applied between two people for a close relationship is basically the same as developing a close relationship with God. That is, for us to understand and develop a closer relationship with God, we must get to know God, in His character, majesty, and splendor better. And the only way we can know Him better is by spending time with Him in His Word, which He has given us in the Bible.

The Bible is replete with inferences that admonish us to be more knowledgeable in our understanding of God through His Word. The following scripture will help us to understand this position:

> "As newborn babes, desires the sincere milk of
> the word, that ye may grow thereby" (1 Peter 2:2)

and

> "So faith cometh by hearing, and hearing by
> the Word of God" (Romans 10:17)

The apostles Peter and Paul wrote during some very distinct times and to some very distinct audiences. Yet both writers valued the importance of Scripture in the life of the believer. If we were to look a little closer at the above-mentioned verses, both Peter and Paul attached great importance to the Word for growing one's personal trust in God through proper understanding (see Proverbs 29:18). Without getting into a lengthy exegetical study of the verses in question, let us put them into perspective by considering our subject matter at hand, if you please.

For any person to come to Christ, they must first exercise a measure of faith (Hebrews 11:6). Once the individual has exercised initial faith, which demands him to believe in the existence of God and to procure his salvation through Christ, there must be a building of that faith, in Christ, by the believer. Hence, a "desire to have the sincere milk of the word, that ye [they] may grow thereby" (1 Peter 2:2).

In other words, for us to develop a more personal relationship with Christ, we must first study His word and learn more about Him (Matthew 11:29). As our faith in God grows, so does our trust of Him, subsequently leading us to a more personal relationship with Him.

The study of God's Word is vitally important in the life of the believer because it gives him a clearer insight into the mind of God. It has always been God's desire to establish consistent but significant relationship with His children. This is apparently seen with Christ saying to his disciples:

> "Abide in me, and I in you. As the branch can-
> not bear fruit of itself, except it abide in the vine; no
> more can ye, except ye abide in me" (John 15:4).

Closeness to God is dependent upon our understanding the very mind of God, which has been revealed in His Word. Faith is dependent upon hearing (and reading) God's Word, along with the proper application to our lives. That is why God calls and demands that we study His word diligently (Deuteronomy 6:4–9).

If we want to successfully draw closer to Him, then we must draw closer to His Word. Why not take a moment and commit your-self to reading and studying God's Word today—it will make a eternal of difference in your life and in your relationship with Him. We need to cherish and nourish God's Word and treat it with such preciousness, seeing that God sent His own Son to die for its fulfillment. The Psalmist wrote, "Thy word is a lamp unto my feet, and a light unto my path" (Ps. 119:105)—that I may draw (or be drawn) closer to you in a more personal way. Job said, "Neither have I gone back from the commandment of his lips; I have esteemed the words of his mouth more than my necessary food" (Job 23:12). Do you value God's Word? You cannot know Him unless you know His Word. I pray the Bible will be a constant presence in your daily life as you seek to draw closer to Him.

Diligence
(I Must Strive)
(Genesis 37–50)

Thus far, we have covered six major steps that I believe are necessary in establishing a more stable and fulfilling relationship with God. In our quest, we have determined that the proper recognition of God and self are extremely important first steps in drawing closer to Him. In addition, we found that with this newfound recognition of God and self comes a clearer and concise understanding of the need for total surrender and obedience by the individuals before he or she could approach God in developing a personal relationship with him. Yet without the proper understanding of God's person, it is virtually impossible to develop a consistent and closer relationship with Him.

I believe that in lieu of the previous action mentioned, to continue drawing closer to God in the development of our personal relationship, we must exercise a high level of diligence; hence, a constant striving to be closer to God.

The scripture is full of individuals, such as Paul, Daniel, and Moses, just to name a few, who gave earnest adherence in keeping the faith and relationship with their Lord, under some unusual circumstances. These individuals faced a matrix of challenges from outright ostracism to the ultimate sacrifice, death. Like the prophet Isaiah, they understood the relationships between God and man and sought to surrender their total being to His service. And yet, when faced with adversity from the world, they gladly and miraculously held their peace and diligently maintained their testimony, even against all odds.

However, today, Christians have focused and concentrated their efforts on things other than that of God. Christians who were once elated about salvation, soul winning, and the good of the church, are now engaged in a constant striving for political, social, and economic agendas, which all too often exclude God. Not knowing that, "No man that warreth entangleth himself with the affairs of this life; that he may please him who hath chosen him to be a soldier" (2 Timothy 2:4). Countless hours and days are exhausted developing, analyzing, and pursuing temporal goods, which "moth and rust doth corrupt, and thieves break through and steal" (Matt. 6:19), instead of laying up eternal treasures in heaven. While diligence in temporal (or non-spiritual) things are not in and of themselves wrong (Prov. 10:4; 12:27; 22:29); it is our prioritizing of these temporal things over spiritual ones that causes the greatest harm and hinders our relationship with God. We must come to understand that a "man's life consisteth not in the abundance of the things which he possesseth" (Luke 12:15). As a matter of fact, we are never compelled by the scripture to draw diligently closer to the things of the world, "but seek ye first the kingdom of God, and His righteousness: and all these things shall be added unto you" (Matt. 6:33).

> *If one is ever going to draw closer to God, he or she must come to realize that as they draw nigh to God, He will draw nigh to them and this is only accomplished through our constant striving to be closer to Him.*

As we have seen, the Bible is full of individuals who have diligently set their hearts to striving toward a closer and more personal relationship with God by having a strict adherence to the Word of

God. One such individual who was constantly mindful of his relationship with God was Joseph.

The life of Joseph, if it were lived today, would be the picture-perfect model of a modern-day soap opera. It was full of sibling rivalry, jealousy, intrigue, murderous plots, manipulation, sexual overtones, lying and falsehood, and the ascent to power (rags to riches), just to name a few. But the underlying factor in Joseph's life was his relationship with His God; nothing else mattered to him, and this is evidently seen in the many struggles he faced. We see a clearer picture of Joseph's determination and diligence in the incident involving Potiphar's wife (Genesis 39:7–9).

When confronted by Potiphar's wife to engage in an illicit relationship, Joseph's thought was immediately turned to his relationship with God and what would be the consequences of such an action on that relationship. Joseph knew that what Potiphar's wife was asking would jeopardize not only his relationship with Potiphar himself, but he asked, "How could I do this great wickedness and sin against God" (Gen. 39:9), which was of paramount importance.

The choice was clear to Joseph, either fall to temptation and ruin his relationship with God or be diligent in his striving to be closer to God and ruin his relationship with Potiphar (and his wife). You would think that the choice would be obvious. But many Christians every day are faced with similar decisions, and unlike Joseph, they succumb to the "lust of the flesh, and the lust of the eyes" (1 John 2:16), because of their failure to apply diligence as a major component in drawing closer to God.

In lieu of his circumstances, Joseph applied an earnest effort in maintaining his closeness to God. He was not easily persuaded to abandon his principles at the first sign of trouble or during constant bombardment of the ill wills of others (39:10). His whole aim was to maintain and draw closer to His God by having diligent and persistent application of principles regardless of the outward circumstances that he faced.

If one is ever to going to draw closer to God, he or she must come to realize that as they draw nigh to God, He will draw nigh to them and this is only accomplished through our constant striving to be closer to Him. If we are easily dislodged or "faint in the day of adversity, [our] thy strength is [said to be] small" (Prov. 24:10). This is all the more reason why it is needful for us to establish and maintain a consistent relationship with the Lord, and this can only be done when we strive to achieve such.

Joseph made the right decision because the Bible declared that "the Lord was with him" (39:23) because of his diligence in drawing nigh to God. Yet most of us will never experience the things faced by Joseph, but how diligent are we in our own trials. Do we automatically think about the consequences of our actions and how they might impact our relationship with God? Well, Joseph did, and I hope you will do the same. We will face many trials and temptations throughout our lifetime, and depending upon our decisions, we will either hinder or help our relationship with God. Diligence in seeking the things of God will be the determining factor in whether we stick close to Him. Take a moment and meditate upon the following verse for future thought:

"But it is good for me to draw nearer to God:
I have put my trust in the Lord God" (Ps. 73:28).

Patience
(Not At My Time)

I believe that the next step in the process of developing a closer relationship with God has to do with our ability to exercise a great level of patience.

Patience is one of those virtues often spoken of and desired but rarely seen or practiced, especially in our society today. As a matter of fact, given the current climate, which prevails in our society today, one could easily conclude that the amount of patience practiced by society is at an all-time low. I need only go back a few years to the advent of the home computer age and the introduction of the 286 and 386 computers, which we believe were the fastest devices in the world (at that time). How, after hitting the power switch, the system would take a few minutes to boot up and then we would be set to start computing; what state-of-the art. Well, as the computer revolution took its course, more powerful machines were introduced that stored more memory and ran ten times faster (486's, Pentium's, and Pentium II, etc.). With the introduction of such powerful machines, we saw our capacity for waiting almost but disappear. We grew less patient with the development and introduction of each computer model and more susceptible to the ills and dictates of our own heart.

While computers and other electronic gadgetry have revolutionized and promoted our standard of living immensely, it appears that one of the main shortfalls of the computer revolution has been its inability to foster our tolerance for patience.

One of the greatest tragedies of our modern society has been our inability to exercise patience as an integral component in our daily relationship with our fellow man. All too often, we hear about individuals taking matters into their own hands because things are not progressing at a suitable pace or according to their own expectations. People are often insulted, injured, or die due to the incapacity of others to practice patience. The Bible is full of stories and admonition that calls upon each of us to develop and walk in patience. In addition, it also details for us the resultant consequences of those who fail to heed this simple but very pertinent command.

> *Patience is one of those virtues often spoken of and desired but rarely seen or practiced, even among God's people.*

There are countless scriptures that call each of us to a higher level of patience, especially when it comes to trusting and developing a closer relationship with God for the direction of our lives. We don't always have the answers to life issues nor do we always know which way to turn when our lives are faced with storms, but if we would but "rest in the Lord, and wait patiently for Him" (Ps. 37:7), then our lives can develop a fuller meaning in our approach and relationship to God. We must come to understand that God's "thoughts are not [our] your thoughts, neither are your ways My [His] ways" (Isaiah 55:8).

By patience, we mean that ability to be steadfast in maintaining our stance or position, and if necessary, to abide or bear up courageously under suffering, regardless of the threat or possible outcome. Hence, it calls for us to direct our energies to someone far greater than our circumstances, knowing that His timing may not always agree with our desired timing. The apostle Paul and James makes mention of developing patience through personal trials when they both wrote:

> "And not only so, but we glory in tribulation also; knowing that tribulation worketh patience. And patience, experience" (Romans 5:3–4).

And

> "Knowing this, that the trying of your faith worketh patience, but let patience have her perfect work" (James 1:3–4).

The perfect work that is developed through patience helps us to draw closer to God by our dependence upon Him. It gives us stability and strengthens our resolve and hope while facing those things which we cannot exercise control over or those things that we cannot see (Rom. 8:25). The development of patience in one's life helps us to submit our imperfect will to God's perfect will. It allows God to have an entrance whereby He can minister to us despite the conditions or injustices that surrounds us.

If we were to perform a self-examination right now of ourselves, how would you rate your level of patience on a scale of one to ten (ten being the highest)? Can you honestly say that when tensions are high or you are faced with an imminent problems, do you exercise or "run with patience" the race that is set before you" (Hebrews 12:1)?" We often hear the clarion cry to get patience, but we must add that after you have obtained it, you must also seek to develop it. It is through this development stage, which is a lifelong process that we can draw closer to God in a personal and meaningful way.

I hope we would come to better understand the importance patience plays in our relationship with our fellow man, but more importantly how it impacts our daily and future relationship with God. We will only draw closer when we patiently believe and submit unto His will for our lives. I hope you will do just that. The prophet Isaiah summarizes this point when he wrote:

> "But they that wait upon the Lord shall renew their strength...
> They shall run, and not be weary; and they shall walk, and not faint" (Isaiah 40:31)

Patience: not at my time, but at His!

Faithfulness:
(Loyalty in Action)

We have successfully completed seven distinct steps I consider are fundamental prerequisites needed for drawing closer to God. However, by no means do we imply or advocate that these steps are the only ones necessary for the achievement of our objective, but I do believe that a person would be hard pressed not to include them as part of his or her overall regiment in developing a personal relationship with God.

Now that we have come to the final section of our study, I am convinced that no study advocating abiding in Christ (or drawing closer to God) would be complete without a brief mentioning of the subject of faithfulness toward God.

The scripture is abounding with examples of God's faithfulness toward His people. However, it also paints a different picture when it comes to man's faithfulness toward God, seeing that God has shown remarkable faithfulness despite our sins and rebellious dispositions. The prophet Jeremiah writes,

> "It is of the Lord's mercies that we are not consumed, because his compassions fail not. They are new every morning: great is thy faithfulness" (Lam. 3:22–23).

Our society is bent on obtaining the most dependable product or faithful service that they can produce. As a matter of fact, dependability is a major marketing tool used by several advertisers and manufacturers. Among those who have pushed the dependability button have been:

a. Timex: "It takes a licking and keeps on ticking."
b. Maytag: "The Dependability People."
c. Chevy Trucks: They are built "Like a Rock."
d. Ford Trucks: "They Are Built Ford Tough."
e. The Energizer Bunny: "It keeps going and going."

It appears that people have gravitated toward these slogans with the expectations that these products are worthy of acceptance because they can be counted on. Hence, dependability is an important sales tool, especially for retaining (brand) loyal customers.

Well, the same principles should be said about our walk with God. For us to draw closer to God, the question is not how faithful God has been to us, but how faithful are we to God in giving of our time, talents, and treasures? Faithfulness, along with dependability and trustworthiness, is something that everyone wants and has come to expect from others, but few are willing to practice it consistently themselves. In other words, we want the best, but very few give their best. So many Christians want the full benefits of God's blessings, but they give minimum or part-time (or no) service to God.

We are admonished to "draw nigh to God" (James 4:8) to allow Him to work through us in the development and personal establishment of a relationship with Him. Of course, this can only be done by the strict adherence through the practicing of diligence based upon the exercising of one's faith in the God of their salvation, and this "faith cometh by hearing, and hearing by the Word of God" (Romans 10:17). It is a known fact that the acquisition of physical nourishment is vital in the support or growth or well-being of all of God's creatures, especially that of mankind, and the lack thereof would only result in stunted growth, the infiltration of diseases due to malnutrition, and ultimately death. Well, similar results can be found in those Christians who refuse to "desire the sincere milk of the word, that ye [they] may grow thereby," i.e., stunted spiritual growth (immaturity), infiltration of diseases (unholy life styles), and even death (prematurely taken away by God).

The mere acquisition of truth is by no means an acknowledgement of one's faithfulness, but it should be the basis of it, i.e., knowing the truth and standing on the truth are two totally different things. The prophet Samuel in his conversation reiterates this point with King Saul: "Hath the Lord as great delight in burnt offerings and sacrifices, as in obeying the voice of the Lord?" (1 Samuel 15:22), and summarized by James in his epistle, "But be ye doers of the word, and not hearers only, deceiving your own selves" (James 1:22).

Faithfulness to God doesn't just happen, it's a process by which one grows continually closer to God as he or she hears (understand) the Word of God; faithfulness becomes the by-product of faith, which has its basis in a committed heart toward the person of Christ. Both Moses and Joshua were two individuals that were committed to the things of God. Each of them faced some unusual circumstances and obstacles in their life in carrying out the will and work of God. I can only imagine the pressures each of these men had to face in lieu of the things God was commanding them to—Moses before Pharaoh and Joshua contending for the Promise Land.

As Moses and Joshua placed their faith in God, they were both given further responsibilities. Hence, their faithfulness in the small things resulted and led to greater trust and responsibility bestowed by God (Luke 19:11–27). Because they believed and trusted God, their relationship to God was greatly established and increased. They remained faithful through the challenges, regardless of the odds that were against them.

Our relationship to God is often hindered or destroyed due to our inability to remain faithful to Him. God demands that we be faithful to Him and the only way this can be accomplished is through the exercising of our faith. We must be committed wholeheartedly to

Him, because "Without faith it is impossible to please Him: for he that cometh to God must believe that He is, and that he is a rewarder of them that diligently seek him" (Hebrews 11:6). If we then lack (growing) faith to approach God, then it would be self-evident that a closer relationship with Him is all but virtually impossible. Moses and Joshua were fully persuaded in what God said, not considering what He did, to draw closer to him. So too are we called upon to develop the same faith and unconditional allegiance to God, regardless of what acts He has displayed or the blessings bestowed but based upon our faith in His Word and His person.

Unless there is diligent effort to strive in developing our faith, then we will never surrender or obey God because of our reservations about him; our lack of diligence may be in part to our unwillingness to seriously draw closer to him in a personal relationship. Again, the question is not whether God is faithful, but have we placed unquestionable faithfulness in the Lord Jesus Christ? Are you willing to be like Moses and Joshua and so many others who exercise a level of faith regardless of the situation? But if you find that your faith is weak and trembling and not able to look beyond your present situation, then be like the father of the demon-possessed son when he cried out and said, "Lord, I believe; help thou mine unbelief" (Mark 9:24).

The Master is willing and ready to draw closer to us the moment we turn and believe in His person. For God commands and demands faith from all His children, especially from those who desire to develop a more personal relationship with Him. Why not take a moment and make a commitment to the Lord right now and ask Him to help you to be more dependable toward Him in giving your life for His service? You will be amazed at what God can do. And be adamant about your relationship with God like Joshua when he concluded: "As for me and my house, we will serve the Lord" (Joshua 24:15).

I hope you will make the same commitment of faithfulness to God and be loyal to Him from this day forward and for evermore. And...

FINAL THOUGHT

I pray that God will help you in your walk with Him. That you might surrender your life to Him in all humility of mind, body, and spirit. And when the storms of life rise, that you will be steadfast and unmovable, always believing and trusting in Him to bring you through.

May the Lord strengthen you and bless you as you read and are drawn closer to Him though this material that you too might be able to testify, "I Have Seen It for Myself."

About The Author

Dr. Victor L. Morrell (BA, MABS, MDiv, DMin) was born February 7, 1958, in Brunswick, Georgia. He is the third and youngest son to the late Aaron David Morrell Jr. and Mrs. Minnie Bell (Morrell) Wright and stepson to Mr. David Wright.

Dr. Morrell is a retired military veteran of the United States Naval Service.

Dr. Morrell is married to the former Carol Lafayette Lawrence and has two adult children: James and Melicia; four grandchildren: twins Terricia and Terrance Jr., Debray, and Jonathan.

Dr. Morrell currently pastors the Trinity Independent Baptist Church in Clinton, Maryland. He is an accomplished leader, soul winner, teacher, and lover of the Lord.

Dr. Morrell presents to you, the reader: *I Have Seen It for Myself.*

CPSIA information can be obtained
at www.ICGtesting.com
Printed in the USA
LVHW030000220221
679537LV00022B/507